CELEBRATING WITH CHILDREN

Liturgical Celebrations for Children Preparing for
the Sacraments of Reconciliation and Eucharist

Joan Brown SND

Kevin Mayhew

First published in 2000 by
KEVIN MAYHEW LTD
Buxhall
Stowmarket
Suffolk
IP14 3BW

© 2000 Joan Brown SND

The right of Joan Brown SND to be identified as the author
of this work has been asserted by her in accordance
with the Copyright, Designs and Patents Act 1988.

The service sheets within this book may be photocopied by the organisation
which purchases this copy without copyright infringement,
provided they are used for the purpose for which they are intended.
Reproduction of any of the contents of this book for commercial purposes
is subject to the usual copyright restrictions.

No other part of this publication may be reproduced,
stored in a retrieval system, or transmitted, in any form or by any means,
electronic, mechanical, photocopying, recording or otherwise,
without the prior permission of the publisher.

All rights reserved.

Scripture quotations are taken from:
The Good News Bible, published by The Bible Societies/HarperCollins Publishers Ltd UK.
© American Bible Society, 1966, 1971, 1976, 1992.

The New Jerusalem Bible, published and © copyright 1985
by Darton, Longman and Todd Ltd and les Editions du Cerf.

0 1 2 3 4 5 6 7 8 9

ISBN 1 84003 481 5
Catalogue No 1500328

Cover design by Jonathan Stroulger
Edited by Helen Elliot
Typesetting by Kevin Whomes

Contents

Introduction	5
The celebrations	5
Using this book	7
Celebrating God's Love and Forgiveness in Advent	9
Service of Reconciliation	13
Celebrating God's Love and Forgiveness in Lent	15
Service of Reconciliation	19
Celebrating God's Gift of Love and Forgiveness	21
Service of Reconciliation	25
Celebration of Enrolment	27
For Preparation for Sacramental Communion	31
Celebration of Illumination	33
Presentation of the Scriptures.	37
Celebration of Tradition	39
Presentation of the Lord's Prayer	43
Celebration at the Crib	45
God with us	49
Celebrating a Meal with Friends	51
Passover/Last Supper/Eucharist	55
Benediction of the Blessed Sacrament	57
Praise and Adoration	59
Celebration of Praise	61
Presentation of First Communion Certificates	

Each celebration begins with an introduction and notes for liturgical leaders *(presiders)* and catechists on how to use the material. Explanatory notes outlining the meaning of the celebration immediately precede each celebration. The complete text of each celebration is clearly set out for the presider. This is followed by a photocopiable leaflet of each celebration, for the use of the congregation.

The material is suitable for use either during Mass or, with the exception of the Benediction of the Blessed Sacrament, as stand-alone services.

The term *presider* is used throughout for *celebrant* or *leader*. The presider may be a priest or lay person depending on the local situation and when and where the celebrations are celebrated.

Introduction

The celebrations contained in this book are intended for children preparing to receive the sacraments of Penance/Reconciliation and Holy Communion for the first time. They are celebrations which involve the children, and in which they can participate with meaningful understanding. The celebrations enable the children to have the experience of belonging to a community of faith: a community which is prepared to take up its responsibility for these children born into it through baptism.

Celebrations in which those present are filled with awareness of and care for each other are celebrations open to God's presence and grace. They are celebrations in which all have the opportunity to grow together, in faith, into a community of love. Community celebrations, such as those presented in this book, help children to understand that, although God knows and loves each of us personally we do not live our faith alone. By faith we are drawn into a community of believers with whom we live and celebrate our belief and find ways to live according to Gospel values.

These celebrations are only one aspect of the preparation of children for their first sacramental celebrations of Penance/Reconciliation and Communion. Catechesis in the faith takes place in the midst of a faith community. During the time of preparation for these sacraments it is important to involve the candidates with the parish community in order that all may reflect on their faith and on the important step the whole community is taking on their spiritual journey.

The Celebrations

Although the celebrations presented in this book are not the same as the Rites of Christian Initiation of Adults (RCIA), the celebrations of Enrolment, Illumination and Tradition are adapted from them. In the first celebration, Enrolment, the candidates for first sacramental communion are called by name and invited to take part, together with their parents and catechist, in a time of preparation for the reception of this sacrament. The community accepts to journey with them by supporting them in prayer.

In the RCIA the period of Enlightenment or Illumination usually falls in Lent in order that the catechumens may prepare themselves for the great feast of Easter and their Baptism. It is a time of purification and a desire to live more closely united with Christ. With the children this period is marked by celebrations of Reconciliation, Illumination and Tradition. In many places children celebrate the sacrament of Penance/Reconciliation for the first time in Lent. If, however, they have celebrated this sacrament earlier, they can be encouraged to take part in the parish celebration of this sacrament in Lent.

In the celebration of Illumination the candidates are presented with a copy of the Gospels so that they may come to know Christ better, love him more dearly and closely follow his way of love. Jesus, the light of the world, is the light of our lives.

In the celebration of Tradition we present the candidates with the Lord's Prayer. This prayer from ancient times has belonged to those who are baptised and who can call God, 'Abba, Father'. It is the prayer which is prayed each time the community gathers. It is the prayer which sums up the teaching of the Gospels and the faith which is handed on to us: the faith which brings us to the altar of God and to eucharist.

Using this Book

Ideally it is better to celebrate these liturgies in a parish context during Mass, but as this may not always be possible, the celebrations can be adapted to meet other situations, perhaps quite simply by substituting the word 'school' or 'classroom' or 'hall' for 'church', and 'assembly' or 'group session' for 'Mass'.

Each celebration begins with an introduction and an explanation for the gathered community of the meaning of what is about to happen. This can be given before the celebration begins. In this way no one is left wondering what is happening. Knowing what is happening and why helps the community to enter more fully into the celebration. The significant moment of each celebration is announced immediately before it takes place. When the celebrations take place at Mass this will be during the Liturgy of the Word.

In order to enhance the meaningfulness of the celebrations for those who participate in them, it is important to prepare them well with the candidates and their families beforehand and to make them as personal as possible. Wherever appropriate, provision is made to address families, children, catechists and parishes by name. Hopefully, celebrating the personal and the community dimension hand in hand will not only give those preparing for the sacraments a sense of belonging to a loving Christian community, but will also help the community to realise their responsibility towards the new life in their midst. It is through sacramental celebration that people become a community of faith.

Since each sacrament deserves its own concentrated preparation, catechesis for the sacrament of Penance/Reconciliation is conducted separately from catechesis for the first celebration of sacramental Communion. Depending on local circumstances, the time of preparation for Penance/Reconciliation varies. In some parishes children may be prepared for Penance/Reconciliation the year previous to their preparation for sacramental Communion or in the term previous to that of communion preparation. Three celebrations for Penance/Reconciliation are therefore offered in this book: one for Advent for children preparing before Christmas for the sacrament of Reconciliation; one for Lent, for children preparing at that time; and a celebration which is not linked to a season and can be used at any time.

Because sacramental preparation is about entering into a loving relationship with Jesus, it is not something that is confined to the contents of a particular programme. As we journey with our children during their time of initiation into the Christian faith, it is vitally important to help them to develop prayer in their lives. We need to help the children to come to know, through prayer, the God who loves them personally; therefore other examples of prayer and adoration are included in this book, in the form of a crib celebration and a Benediction of the Blessed Sacrament.

During their time of preparation it is also helpful to draw the children's attention to the seasons and feasts of the Church's year.

For each celebration in this book a full copy of the text is given for the presider, and there are service sheets, which you may photocopy, for the congregation. Readings and hymns are suggested for the celebrations, but are not included on the service sheets as you might like to choose your own. The hymns and carols suggested can be found in *Our songs*, published by Kevin Mayhew, with the exception of those printed in full on the service sheet.

Although the celebrations contained in this book are linked to the children's preparation material in my books, *Loved and forgiven* and *Meet Christ with joy*, their use is not limited to this material. It is not the purpose of these celebrations to fit in with programmes. The celebrations of the various stages of Initiation based on the RCIA rites, that is, Enrolment, Tradition and Illumination, can be used with any home-, school- or parish-based sacramental preparation. Other opportunities for prayer and celebrations at home and in catechetical groups are offered in *Loved and forgiven* and *Meet Christ with joy*.

Celebrating God's Love and Forgiveness

A celebration of Reconciliation in Advent

Introduction

The celebration begins with the church in darkness and soft music playing. When all are seated one child enters, carrying a large lighted candle. The child enters the sanctuary, turns to face the congregation and holds the candle up high. A second child will carry in the figure of the infant Jesus from the crib. A third child will carry in the Bible, the Word of God, accompanied by two or more candle bearers.

During Advent we celebrate the end of a long dark night of waiting and the dawning of a new day, the dawning of the Lord's coming and, with him, the everlasting day. We celebrate the coming of the Light of the world, the light foretold by God's messenger, John, who shone so brightly himself he was thought to be that light, but he had come to tell the people about the true light which would give light to everyone in the world. During Advent, as we watch and wait with hope for the coming of the Lord, we pray that God may increase in us the strength of will to do good, and remove from us the things that hinder us from receiving Christ joyfully into our lives, now that we will be one with him when he comes in glory.

Preparation

You will need:
- *Bible or lectionary*
- *Disc/tapes and player for music*
- *Large candle for opening of celebration*
- *Stand for large candle, placed in front of the altar*
- *Candle for each family present*
- *Stand(s) in or near sanctuary for family candles, or pots of sand*
- *Two or more candles for Gospel procession*
- *Candle for each penitent*
- *Dishes or stands for penitents' candles (place penitents' candles around manger; penitents' candles will be extinguished and re-lighted during the celebration)*
- *As many other candles as wished*
- *Figure of the infant Jesus from the crib*
- *Manger from the crib, placed in front of the large candle stand*
- *Matches and tapers*
- *Candle extinguisher(s)*
- *Crucifix for each first-time penitent (choice of parents)*
- *Table on which to place crucifixes*
- *Holy water for blessing of crucifixes*
- *Rite of blessing*
- *Selection of carols*

Celebrating God's Love and Forgiveness in Advent

Child enters carrying a large lighted candle. Processes to the sanctuary, turns to face the congregation and holds the candle up.
Children then say:

(Children) The world was in darkness, nobody knew the way to our Father; you and I do.
They needed a light to show them the way;
that great light shone, Jesus was born on Christmas Day.

The candle is placed in the stand by an adult.

Welcome and introduction

Presider   Welcome to our Advent celebration of Reconciliation. During Advent we remember the time when Jesus, the Son of God, the light of the world, was born into our world many years ago, but we think of Jesus always with us now, and, in this special celebration, the children will be meeting him for the first time in the sacrament of Reconciliation. We also look forward to the time when Jesus will return in glory. Certain that Jesus will come, we want to be ready, awake and on the watch, because we do not know when he will come. A few minutes ago a candle was carried into the dark church and we read a poem. The poem told us that, before Jesus was born, the world was in darkness and nobody knew the way to our Father God. The people needed a light to show them the way to God. Jesus, born on Christmas Day, is the great light showing us the way to God. Each time we celebrate the sacrament of Reconciliation, the light of Jesus comes into our lives, lighting up our way, helping us to remember and be ready for the time when Jesus will return in glory. As a sign that we want to be filled with the light of Jesus each family is now invited to come forward to light a candle from the large candle.

Lighting of family candles

During the singing of the following song each family comes forward and lights a candle from the large candle.

Song   Thank you for giving us your light, Lord.
Thank you for lighting up our way.
Thank you that we can find
our way now, safely home to you.

Thank you, you light up all our darkness.
Thank you for being born for us.
Thank you for teaching us to live
in kindness and in love.

Thank you that we can be your candles.
Thank you for every family here.
Thank you that we can shine out brightly in love and harmony.

Thank you that we can be Christ's bright light.
Thank you that all the world can see.
Thank you for all the shining
of Christ's light in you and me.

Thank you that you will come again, Lord.
Thank you that we can hope in you.
Thank you for all the signs you give which help us to believe.

(Tune 'Thank you for giving us each morning'.)

Repeat as necessary or add another song or carol such as 'O little town of Bethlehem'.

When all the candles have been lit:

Presider   When we arrived it was quite dark in the church. Then one tiny little light was carried in. From that one little light all these other lights have been lit. Each time we lit a candle, the church became brighter and brighter, and now it is all lit up. The first candle did not lose any of its light by sharing it, it is just as bright as ever. But, because it shared its light, the church has become brighter and brighter. God gave us Jesus to be the light of the world. When we share the light of Jesus we make our world brighter.

During the singing of the next carol one child carries in the figure of the infant Jesus. The child enters the sanctuary, holds up the 'infant' for all to see and then places it in the manger.

Hymn   'O come, all ye faithful' (verses 1 and 3) or another suitable carol.

Prayer

Presider   Heavenly Father, we pray that these children preparing to celebrate this most wonderful sacrament of your love and forgiveness today, will be filled with the light of Jesus, your Son, who came on earth to live with us. May the love of Jesus be a light to the whole world and shine out through us in all we think and do and say. Amen.

Song to welcome the Gospel
'Lord, the light of your love is shining' or a suitable hymn of choice.

During the singing of the song one child, accompanied by two or more acolytes carrying lighted candles, processes the book of the Gospel down the church to the lectern.

Gospel reading

Presider   The Lord be with you.
All   And also with you.

Reader   A reading from the Holy Gospel given to us by St John, chapter 1 verses 6-10.
All   Glory to you, Lord.

God sent his messenger, a man named John, who came to *tell* the people about the light, so that everyone would hear the message and believe. John was not the light: he only came to tell the people about the light; the real light that comes into the world and shines on all peoples. The light shines in the darkness and the darkness has never put it out.

Reader   This is the Gospel of the Lord.
All   Praise to you, Lord Jesus Christ.

Homily

Examination of conscience

Presider   Jesus is the light of the world. The light of Jesus can shine out brightly through us. With every loving and kind, honest and true action we do the light of Jesus shines more brightly in our lives.

Invite the children to name actions which increase the light. For each action named, a penitent places a candle in front of the manger which is lighted by an adult.

Presider   As we prepare for Christmas, we remember the great gift of love God gave us by sending us Jesus on the first Christmas night. How have we shared God's gift of love with our families and friends? We are now going to be quiet for a little while to think of times when we have not helped to spread the light and love of Jesus at home, at school, at play.

If we block out the light of Jesus we are left in the dark.

Invite the children to name some of the ways in which we can block the light of Jesus. For each way named an adult extinguishes a candle in front of the manger.

Presider   For any times we have not helped the light of Jesus to shine let us say we are sorry.

Prayer of Sorrow

Children   O my God, my loving Father,
            I am sorry for all my sins,
            I am sorry for not loving other
                people and for not loving you.
            Help me to live in the light as
                Jesus came to show me,
            and help me not to sin again.
            Amen.

Individual confessions with absolution.
During this time carols can be played. After confessing, each child, helped by an adult, re-lights a candle in front of the manger.

Blessing and distribution of crucifixes
After the confessions have been completed the crucifixes are blessed. The children are invited to come forward. A crucifix is given to each child with the words:

(Presider) Receive the cross of Jesus Christ, our Lord, a sign of his everlasting love for you.

Closing blessing

Presider   Go in peace to love one another as Jesus taught us.
All   Amen.

Presider   Go in peace to be a light for the world.
All   Amen.

Presider   Go in peace to spread the love and joy of Christmas.
All   Amen.

Presider   May Almighty God bless us all, Father, Son and Holy Spirit.
All   Amen.

Closing hymn or carol of choice.

CELEBRATING

God's Love and Forgiveness in Advent

Individual confessions with absolution
During this time carols can be played.

After confessing each child helped by an adult, re-lights a candle in front of the manger.

Blessing and distribution of crucifixes
After the confessions have been completed the crucifixes are blessed. The children are invited to come forward. A crucifix is given to each child with the words:

(Presider) Receive the cross of Jesus Christ, our Lord,
a sign of his everlasting love for you.

Closing blessing

Presider Go in peace to love one another as Jesus taught us.
All Amen.

Presider Go in peace to be a light for the world.
All Amen.

Presider Go in peace to spread the love and joy of Christmas.
All Amen.

Presider May Almighty God bless us all,
Father, Son and Holy Spirit.
All Amen.

Closing hymn or choice of carol.

Child enters carrying a large lighted candle. Processes to the sanctuary. Turns to face the congregation and holds up the candle.

Children The world was in darkness, nobody knew the way to our Father, you and I do.
They needed a light to show them the way; that great light shone, Jesus was born on Christmas Day.

Welcome and introduction

Lighting of family candles during the song.

Song Thank you for giving us your light, Lord.
Thank you for lighting up our way.
Thank you that we can find our way now safely home to you.

Thank you, you light up all our darkness.
Thank you for being born for us.
Thank you for teaching us to live in kindness and in love.

Thank you that we can be your candles.
Thank you for every family here.
Thank you that we can shine out brightly in love and harmony.

Thank you that we can be Christ's bright light.
Thank you that all the world can see.
Thank you for all the shining of Christ's light in you and me.

Thank you that you will come again, Lord.
Thank you that we can hope in you.
Thank you for all the signs you give which help us to believe.

Repeat as necessary or add song or carol of choice.

Address to the penitents

During the next carol a child carries in the figure of the infant Jesus, enters the sanctuary, holds the 'infant' high, then places it in the manger.

Hymn 'O come, all ye faithful' (verses 1 and 3) or carol of choice.

Prayer

Song to welcome the Gospel
'Lord, the light of your love is shining', or carol of choice.

During the singing of this song one child, accompanied by acolytes carrying lighted candles, processes the book of the Gospel to the lectern.

Gospel reading: John 1:6-10

Homily followed by examination of conscience

Prayer of sorrow
Children O my God, my loving Father, I am sorry for all my sins, I am sorry for not loving other people and for not loving you. Help me to live in the light as Jesus came to show me, and help me not to sin again.
All Amen.

Celebrating God's Love and Forgiveness

A celebration of Reconciliation in Lent

Introduction

This celebration begins with the penitents processing into the church. A large crucifix is carried high at the head of the procession. The cross-bearer enters the sanctuary, turns to face the congregation and raises the cross then places it in position. Penitents go to their places. Acolytes with lighted candles will accompany the book in the Gospel procession.

Lent is a time for recognising our need for help. Lent is a time for calling out to God in our need: 'Lord, remember me?' Lent is a time for coming face to face with the wonder of God's love and goodness: 'I forgive you...'

> Even when we disobeyed you and lost your friendship you did not abandon us to the power of death... again and again you offered us a covenant...
>
> Eucharist prayer IV, Roman Missal

Lent is a time for having clean water poured over us, a time of new life in the Spirit.

> I shall pour clean water over you
>   and you will be cleansed;
> I shall cleanse you of all your defilement
>   and all your idols.
> I shall give you a new heart,
>   and put a new spirit in you;
> I shall remove your heart of stone
>   and give you a heart of flesh instead.
>
> Ezekiel 36:25-27

The first effect of God's gift of love is the forgiveness of our sin, new life in Christ. We are not condemned, we are not treated as our sins deserve...'Today you will be with me in Paradise,' says Jesus.

Preparation

You will need:
- Discs or tapes and player for music
- Large crucifix and stand in which to place the crucifix in front of the altar
- Candles for Gospel procession
- Bible or lectionary
- Night-light for each penitent
- Taper and matches
- Crucifix for each first-time penitent
- Table on which to place the crucifixes
- Holy water for blessing the crucifixes
- Rite of blessing

Depending on the size of the group and the funds available, adapt the type of cross or crucifix presented, for example a picture, a small cross on a cord to place round the neck, a standing or wall crucifix, a cut-out paper or card cross.

Celebrating God's Love and Forgiveness in Lent

Procession of first-time penitents enters, led by the crucifix. Only the cross-bearer enters the sanctuary. The cross is raised high for all to see and then placed in position.

Hymn   Lenten hymn of choice

Welcome and introduction

Presider   Welcome to our celebration of God's love and forgiveness. This is a special occasion for our children who will be experiencing Jesus' love for them in the sacrament of Penance and Reconciliation during this celebration; a celebration which began with the penitents following the cross of Jesus into the church, the holy cross on which Jesus died to save the world, to save each one of us. The cross is the great sign of Jesus' love for us. Could anyone love us more? And so we dare to come today to ask forgiveness, knowing that we will be forgiven, because we are loved so much. In fact we already are forgiven.

Hymn   Thank you, O Lord, your love is boundless.
Thank you, you gave your life for me.
Thank you, that I can be forgiven and live life new with you.

(Tune: 'Thank you for giving us each morning.')

Prayer

Presider   Loving Father, we pray that these children preparing to celebrate this most wonderful sacrament of your love and forgiveness will be filled with the Spirit of your Son Jesus who, filled with your love, laid down his life for his friends. We pray that our selfishness may be changed into self-giving, our sadness into joy, as we prepare to glory in the new life of Easter. We make our prayer through Jesus Christ, our Lord. Amen.

Song to welcome the Gospel
'Lord of the dance', verse 1 and refrain.

During the singing of the hymn children carrying lighted candles accompany the procession of the book to the lectern.

Gospel reading

Presider   The Lord be with you.
All   And also with you.

Reader   A reading from the Holy Gospel given to us by St Luke, ch. 23:39-43.
All   Glory to you, Lord.

The Good Thief
Before he died on the cross on Calvary, Jesus did something very wonderful. Fastened on crosses on either side of Jesus were two thieves. One of them began to mock Jesus: 'If you are who you say you are, why don't you work one of your miracles and save yourself and us as well?' The other thief spoke up and told him off. 'Have you no fear of God at all? We were given the same sentence as Jesus, but we deserved it. We are paying for our wickedness, Jesus has not done anything wrong.' Turning to Jesus he said, 'Lord, remember me when you come into your kingdom.' Jesus said, 'I promise you, today you will be with me in paradise.'

This is the Gospel of the Lord.

Invitation to venerate the figure of Jesus on the cross

Presider   This is the wood of the cross on which hung the Saviour of the world.
All   Come let us worship.

Taizé music, such as 'Jesus, remember me, when you come into your kingdom', or similar is played while the children receiving the sacrament for the first time come forward to venerate the figure of Jesus on the cross in their own way. Other members of the congregation may follow if they wish to do so. In this service of Reconciliation it is not the cross which is venerated as on Good Friday, but the figure of Jesus whose arms are stretched out wide on the cross in love for us. The crucifix may be held by two people.

Examination of conscience

Presider Jesus came to set us free; to show us how to be happy, not just today, but now and for ever. He shared his secret for happiness with us: 'Love one another as I love you.' We know how much Jesus loves us and wants us to share his love with others. Instead we sometimes choose to be unhappy and to make our families and friends unhappy.

Let us remember the times when we have chosen to make others unhappy
    by fighting and quarrelling,
    by telling lies,
    by spoiling or damaging things that are not ours.

Lord have mercy.
Children Lord have mercy.

Presider Let us remember the times when we have chosen to make others unhappy
    by our selfishness and bad temper,
    by being spiteful and jealous,
    by sulking.

Christ have mercy.
Children Christ have mercy.

Presider Let us remember the times when we have chosen to make others unhappy
    by our laziness,
    by not doing our share of work at home,
    by being rude and bad mannered.

Lord have mercy.
Children Lord have mercy.

Presider Let us be quiet and in our hearts ask Jesus to help us and to forgive all our sins.

Prayer of sorrow

Children God, my loving Father,
I am sorry for all my sins.
I am sorry for not loving
    other people
and for not loving you.
Help me to live in love
    as Jesus came to show me,
and give me your help
    not to sin again. Amen.

Individual confessions with absolution

During this time soft background music such as Taizé can be played. After confessing each child lights a night-light and places it in front of the crucifix before returning to their place.

Blessing and distribution of crucifixes

After the confessions have been completed the crucifixes are blessed. The children are invited to come forward. A crucifix is given to each child with the words:

(Presider) Receive the cross of Jesus Christ, our Lord, a sign of his everlasting love for you.

Closing blessing

Presider Go in peace to love one another as Jesus taught us.
All Amen.

Presider Go in peace to be a light for the world.
All Amen.

Presider Go in peace to spread the love and joy of Jesus.
All Amen.

Presider May Almighty God bless us all, Father, Son and Holy Spirit.
All Amen.

Final hymn

CELEBRATING

God's Love and Forgiveness in Lent

Individual confessions with absolution

After confessing each child lights a night-light and places it in front of the crucifix before returning to their place.

Hymn

Blessing and distribution of crucifixes

When the confessions are completed each child is invited to come forward and receive a blessed crucifix.

Presider Receive the cross of Jesus Christ, our Lord,
a sign of his everlasting love for you.

Closing blessing

Presider Go in peace to love one another as Jesus taught us.
All Amen.

Presider Go in peace to be a light for the world.
All Amen.

Presider Go in peace to spread the love and joy of Jesus.
All Amen.

Presider May Almighty God bless us all,
Father, Son and Holy Spirit.
All Amen.

Closing hymn

Procession of first-time penitents enters, led by the crucifix.

Opening hymn

Welcome and introduction

Hymn   Thank you, O Lord, your love is boundless.
Thank you, you gave your life for me.
Thank you, that I can be forgiven
and live life new with you.

Prayer

Song to welcome the Gospel

St Luke 23:39-43, The Good Thief.

Invitation to venerate the figure of Jesus on the cross

Presider   This is the wood of the cross on which hung the Saviour of the world.

All   Come let us worship.

Children receiving the sacrament for the first time come forward first to venerate the figure of Jesus on the cross in their own way. Members of the congregation may follow if they wish to do so.

Examination of conscience

Presider   Let us remember the times when we have chosen to make others unhappy by fighting and quarrelling, by telling lies, by spoiling or damaging things that are not ours.

Children   Lord have mercy.
Lord have mercy.

Presider   Let us remember the times when we have chosen to make others unhappy by our selfishness and bad temper, by being spiteful and jealous, by sulking.

Children   Christ have mercy.
Christ have mercy.

Presider   Let us remember the times when we have chosen to make others unhappy by our laziness, by not doing our share of work at home, by being rude and bad mannered.

Children   Lord have mercy.
Lord have mercy.

Moment of quiet reflection

Prayer of sorrow

Children   God, my loving Father,
I am sorry for all my sins.
I am sorry for not loving other people
and for not loving you.
Help me to live in love as Jesus came to show me,
and give me your help not to sin again.
Amen.

Celebrating God's Gift of Love and Forgiveness

Introduction

This celebration of Reconciliation is for use outside the seasons of Advent and Lent.

Reconciliation is at the heart of the Gospel. Jesus came to bring peace upon earth. He came to reconcile human beings with each other and with God. From earliest times Christian communities have made great efforts to be communities of forgiveness and reconciliation: to live what Jesus taught us, to pray in the Lord's Prayer, 'Forgive us our trespasses as we forgive those who trespass against us'.

We read in the Catechism of the Catholic Church, Nos. 1420 and 1421, that we receive new life in Christ through the sacraments of baptism, confirmation and the eucharist, but we carry this life 'in earthen vessels'. It is new life as a child of God, it can be weakened and even lost by sin. But our Lord, Jesus Christ, has given to his Church the power of the Holy Spirit to continue his work of healing and salvation, work which is continued in the sacraments of penance and the anointing of the sick.

There is no limit or measure to God's forgiveness as we hear over and over again in the scriptures. God's forgiveness is a love that has no end. We can pray with confidence for the forgiveness of our trespasses in the Lord's Prayer, knowing that we are forgiven even before we ask, because with God nothing is impossible. But we also ask in this prayer to be forgiven 'as we forgive those who trespass against us'. We are asking for help to live the new commandment of Christ, 'Love one another as I have loved you…', even our enemies. If we harden our hearts against our brothers and sisters we prevent the merciful love of God from entering them.

It is important, therefore, to help the children to realise how special they are to God, how loved they are by God, and how God's limitless power and love are always there for them. This sacrament has many names, but whatever name it goes by it will always be the sacrament of limitless love. The sacrament of love that knows no end: God's love for us, our love for God and our love for each other, including our enemies.

Preparation

Create a focal point, perhaps using the paschal candle, or pictures of the children taking part in the celebration, or a bowl of water, reminding the children of their baptism.

You will also need:
Book of the Gospel
Two candles, matches and taper
Service sheets with choice of hymns
Cassette player and music cassettes for playing during the time of individual confession
Crucifix or cross for each child if this is their first celebration of the sacrament
Table on which to place the crucifixes
Holy water for blessing of crucifixes
Rite of Blessing

If this celebration is used other than for first Reconciliation omit the blessing and distribution of the crucifixes.

Celebrating God's Gift of Love and Forgiveness

Welcome and introduction

Children   I am special to God who loves me very much. When I was baptised I was welcomed into God's very own family. I am God's special child.

Opening hymn *(of choice)*

Children   Loving God,
Thank you for welcoming me
   into your family.
Thank you for giving me
   this beautiful world to live in.
Thank you for my family
   and my friends.
Thank you for making me.
Thank you for calling me
   by my name.
Thank you for the wonderful
   things I can do.
Thank you most of all
   for loving me.

Sung Gospel acclamation or alleluia

A reading from the holy Gospel
(Scripture reading of choice.)

Repeat acclamation or alleluia

Homily

Examination of conscience

Presider   Let us remember and be sorry for: the times we have not been welcoming;
Children   Lord have mercy.

Presider   the times we did not take care of our beautiful world;
Children   Lord have mercy.

Presider   the times we have been unkind and unloving to our family and friends;
Children   Lord have mercy.

Presider   the times we have not been thankful and have spoilt things for others.
Children   Lord have mercy.

Children   Loving God, help us to live and love and share like Jesus who says: 'Do not be afraid, I will always love you.'

Prayer of sorrow

Children   God, my Father,
   thank you for loving me.
I am sorry for my sins.
I am sorry for not loving other
   people and for not loving you.
Help me to live as Jesus came to
   show me,
and help me not to sin again.
Amen.

Children   Like the shepherd who searched for the sheep that was lost, like the woman who looked for her coin. Like the father who welcomed his son back home and prepared a great feast in his name. Like the thief on the cross whom Jesus forgave, I will always trust and believe in God's love for me.

Individual confessions

Blessing and distribution of crucifixes

After the confessions have been completed the crucifixes are blessed. The children are invited to come forward. A crucifix is given to each child with the words:

(Presider) Receive the cross of Jesus Christ, our Lord,
a sign of his everlasting love for you.

Prayer of praise and thanksgiving

Children   Loving Father God,
I praise and thank you.
You are great and you are wonderful.
Thank you for sending Jesus
to be my friend and to help me.
Thank you for sending your Holy
Spirit to make me strong.
Thank you for forgiving my sins
and for loving me for ever.

Final blessing

Presider   May almighty God bless you and keep you from all harm.
Children   Amen.

Presider   May God look upon you with kindness and fill you with peace.
Children   Amen.

Presider   May you always walk in the way of God's love.
Children   Amen.

Presider   May almighty God bless you, the Father, the Son and the Holy Spirit.
Children   Amen.

Closing hymn *(of choice)*

child with the words:

Presider Receive the cross of Jesus Christ, our Lord,
a sign of his everlasting love for you.

Prayer of praise and thanksgiving

Children Loving Father God, I praise and thank you.
You are great and you are wonderful.
Thank you for sending Jesus
to be my friend and to help me.
Thank you for sending your Holy Spirit
to make me strong.
Thank you for forgiving my sins
and for loving me for ever.

Final Blessing

Presider May almighty God bless you
and keep you from all harm.
Children Amen.

Presider May God look upon you with kindness
and fill you with peace.
Children Amen.

Presider May you always walk in the way of God's love.
Children Amen.

Presider May almighty God bless you,
the Father, the Son and the Holy Spirit.
Children Amen.

CELEBRATING

God's Gift of Love and Forgiveness

Welcome and introduction

Children I am special to God who loves me very much. When I was baptised I was welcomed into God's very own family. I am God's special child.

Opening hymn

Children Loving God,
thank you for welcoming me into your family.
Thank you for giving me this beautiful world to live in.
Thank you for my family and my friends.
Thank you for making me.
Thank you for calling me by my name.
Thank you for the wonderful things I can do.
Thank you most of all for loving me.

Gospel acclamation or alleluia

A reading from the holy Gospel…

Repeat acclamation or alleluia

Homily

Examination of conscience

Presider Let us remember and be sorry for:
the times we have not been welcoming;
Children Lord have mercy.

Presider the times we did not take care of our beautiful world;
Children Lord have mercy.

Presider the times we have been unkind and unloving to our family and friends;
Children Lord have mercy.

Presider the times we have not been thankful and have spoilt things for others.
Children Lord have mercy.

Children Loving God, help us to live and love and share like Jesus who says: 'Do not be afraid, I will always love you.'

Prayer of sorrow

Children God, my Father, thank you for loving me.
I am sorry for my sins. I am sorry for not loving other people and for not loving you. Help me to live as Jesus came to show me. And help me not to sin again. Amen.

Children Like the shepherd who searched for the sheep that was lost; like the woman who looked for her coin.
Like the father who welcomed his son back home and prepared a great feast in his name.
Like the thief on the cross whom Jesus forgave,
I will always trust and believe in God's love for me.

Individual confessions

After the confessions have been completed the crucifixes are blessed. The children are invited to come forward. A crucifix is given to each

Celebration of Enrolment of Candidates for Eucharist

The presentation of the candidates

Introduction

At this celebration we welcome our children who wish to be accepted as candidates for preparation for their first sacramental celebration of Holy Communion.

During the celebration the candidates will give their names to the presider who will receive them on behalf of the Christian community. The candidates may also be presented with the materials they will be using during their time of preparation. Parents, catechists and the community are invited to commit themselves to the support and preparation of the candidates.

When celebrated during Mass, the Rite of Enrolment takes place after the homily.

Preparation

You will need:
- *List of names of the families*
- *List of names of the candidates*
- *Name card for each candidate on which their name is clearly printed*
- *Any materials to be presented to the candidates*
- *Service sheets for the congregation*

CELEBRATING WITH CHILDREN

The Celebration of Enrolment

Introduction

Initiated into the family of God, the Christian community, through baptism, the candidates wishing to prepare to receive Jesus in Holy Communion belong to and already have a place within our community, which welcomed them with great joy at their baptism.

In this Rite of Enrolment the members of the Christian community are called to remember the joyful welcome with which they greeted these candidates at their baptism and to welcome them once more as they prepare for their first celebration of Holy Communion. The community is invited to pray for them, and to support them and their families, on the strength of the faith they profess, by trying to live the way of love as Jesus showed us.

Welcome

Presider   Parents and candidates for first Holy Communion, in the name of our Lord Jesus Christ, and in the name of his people gathered here, I welcome you to this celebration of enrolment for first Holy Communion and invite you to stand and express the desire of your hearts.

Catechist calls each family by name. Families stand as they are named.

Presider   Parents, what is the name of your child?

Parents in turn say aloud the name their child.

Presider   Parents, what do you ask of God's Church for your children?

Parents   Holy Communion.

Presider   Parents, you have asked to have your child prepared to receive Jesus in Holy Communion. In doing so you are accepting the responsibility of helping them to grow in the practice and understanding of the faith, in the love of God, and of one another as Jesus showed us. Do you understand what you are undertaking?

Parents   We do.

Presider   In the name of the Christian community I sign you with the cross of Christ. By this sign of his love Christ will be your strength.

Parents either come forward individually or celebrant blesses the group.

Parents   Amen.

Presider   Parents, I now ask you in the name of the faith community to bless your children by tracing the cross of Christ on their foreheads as you did at their baptism.

Parents sign their children with the sign of the cross.

Presider   We now invite our candidates for first Holy Communion to come forward.

Catechist reads out the names of the candidates. Candidates come to the edge of the sanctuary.

Presider   Dear candidates, do you wish to receive Jesus in the Sacrament of Holy Communion?

Candidates   We do.

Presider   Please give me your names.

Candidates come forward one by one and give the presider their name card. Presider receives the name card and, placing a hand on the child's head, says:

(Presider)   N…*(name of child)*, I now accept you as a candidate for Holy Communion.

Children remain in the sanctuary.

Presider Members of…(name of parish), will you support these parents with your prayers and faith as they help to prepare their children to receive Jesus in Holy Communion?

All We will.

Presider Catechists, will you work faithfully to prepare these children to the best of your ability for their first celebration of Holy Communion?

Catechists We will.

Prayer

Presider Let us pray.

Loving Father, we thank you for these children who today have asked to be accepted as candidates for Holy Communion. We welcome them among us and ask you to increase their faith in Jesus and their love of him.

Help us to be a support and inspiration to them by the example of our following of Christ. We make our prayer through Jesus Christ, our Lord. Amen.

The presider may now present each candidate with a copy of the book they will be using for their preparation. They then return to their families.

Intercessions

Presider The greatest of all gifts is love. We are a community of faith, of hope, but above all of love.

As we today enrol our candidates preparing for their first celebration of Holy Communion, the great sacrament of love, we pray for them that through the love of this community they may experience the love of Christ.

We pray for the families of our candidates, especially for their parents who first brought these children to Christ in baptism and who are now presenting them for preparation for Holy Communion. May this be a time of strengthening and deepening of their own faith.

We pray for our catechists who have accepted the responsibility of helping these parents to prepare their children for Holy Communion. May their lives be always centred on Christ whose Good News they proclaim.

We pray for our parish family who have undertaken to support these candidates, their families and the catechists with their prayers. May we be living witnesses for them of the love of Christ.

We pray for the sick and housebound of our parish family and for our eucharist ministers who bring Christ to them in Holy Communion.

We pray for those who have departed this life, especially our relatives and friends, that they may now be enjoying the full communion of love with Christ in heaven.

Other intercessions may be added.

CELEBRATION of Enrolment

Presider Catechists, will you work faithfully to prepare these children to the best of your ability for their first celebration of Holy Communion?

Catechists We will.

Prayer

The presider may now present each candidate with a copy of the book they will be using for their preparation. They then return to their families.

Intercessions

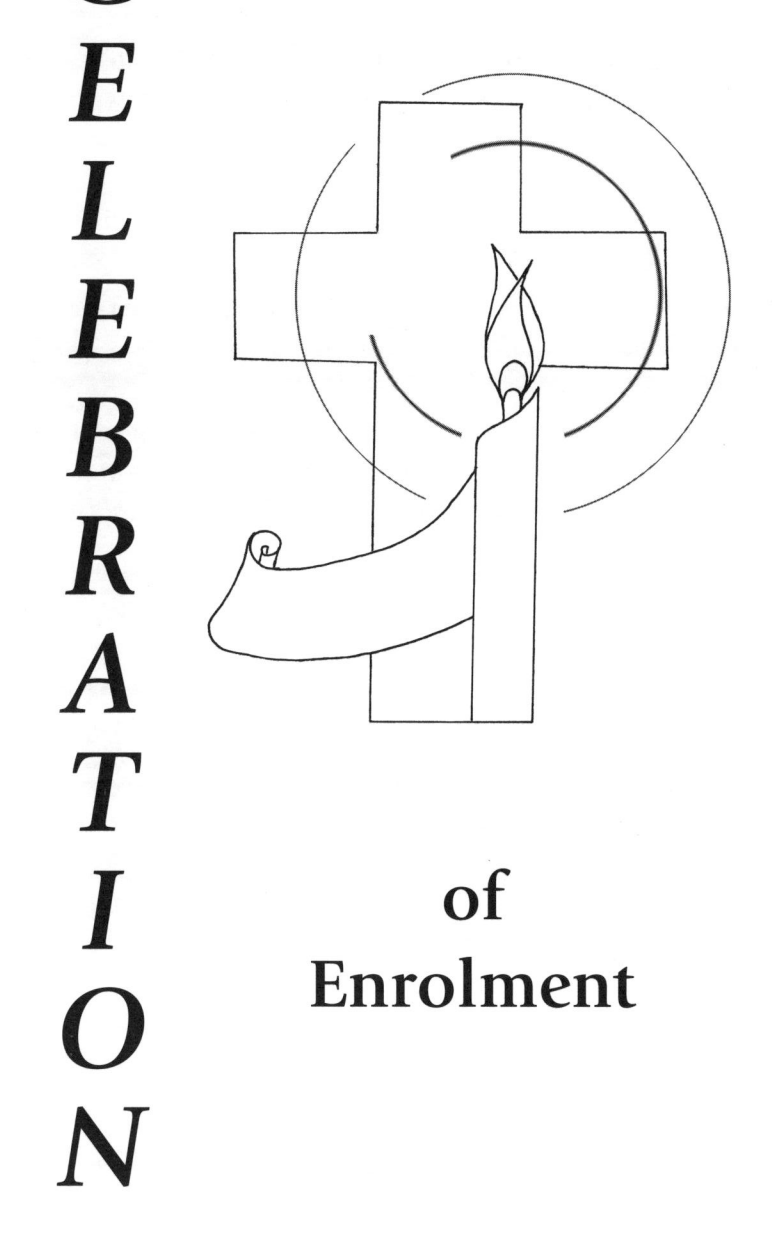

Welcome and introduction

Catechist calls each family by name. Families stand as they are named.

Presider   Parents, what is the name of your child?

Parents in turn say aloud the name their child.

Presider   Parents, what do you ask of God's Church for your children?

Parents   Holy Communion.

Presider   Parents, you have asked to have your child prepared to receive Jesus in Holy Communion. In doing so you are accepting the responsibility of helping them to grow in the practice and understanding of the faith, in the love of God and one another as Jesus showed us. Do you understand what you are undertaking?

Parents   We do.

Presider   In the name of the Christian community I sign you with the cross of Christ. By this sign of his love Christ will be your strength.

Parents either come forward individually or presider signs the group.

Parents   Amen.

Presider   Parents, I now invite you, in the name of the faith community, to bless your children by tracing the cross of Christ on their foreheads as you did at their baptism.

Parents sign their children with the sign of the cross.

Presider   We now invite our candidates for first Holy Communion to come forward.

Catechist reads out the names of the candidates. Candidates come to the edge of the sanctuary.

Presider   Dear candidates, do you wish to receive Jesus in the sacrament of Holy Communion?

Candidates   We do.

Presider   Please give me your names.

Candidates come forward into the sanctuary one by one and give their name card to the presider. Presider receives the name card and, placing a hand on the child's head, says:

(Presider)   N … (name of child), I now accept you as a candidate for Holy Communion.

Children remain in the sanctuary.

Presider   Members of … (name of parish), will you support these parents with your prayers and faith as they help to prepare their children to receive Jesus in Holy Communion?

All   We will.

CELEBRATION OF ILLUMINATION

The Presentation of the Scriptures

Introduction

The Rite of the Presentation of the Scriptures takes place after the homily when it is celebrated during Mass, but the candidates are welcomed at the beginning of the Mass. The Rite begins with prayer for the candidates for sacramental Communion. If celebrated outside the Mass, the Gospel and the Rite of the Presentation of the Scriptures will immediately follow the greeting and suitable hymns or music may be included.

Preparation

You will need:
- *Lighted candles to be carried by acolytes*
- *Paschal candle to be placed beside the ambo*
- *Baptismal candle to show the children*
- *Holy water*
- *Copies of the Synoptic Gospel of the current year, or New Testaments or Bibles for each candidate*
- *Table on which to place the books*
- *Gospel acclamation or Alleluia set to music*
- *Candles or night-lights for the candidates (optional)*
- *Matches and taper*
- *Gathering music or song and a recessional song or hymn for the Rite if celebrated outside Mass*

The Celebration of Illumination

Introduction

At this celebration we again welcome our children who are preparing to receive Jesus for the first time in Holy Communion. To help these children as they journey in faith towards this sacrament we will present them today with a book of the Holy Gospel, the living Word of God's everlasting love, Jesus. As we journey through life we want the Word of God to light up our way, to be a lamp for our feet and a light on our path. This is why we call this presentation of the Word of God, a 'Celebration of Illumination'.

Presider's greeting *(at the beginning of Mass)*

> Children, in the name of our Lord Jesus Christ and in the name of all who believe in him and are here today, we welcome you to celebrate the gift of God's Word to us in the Scriptures. Today you are invited to take part in a service of light. At your baptism your parents received a lighted candle in your name, your baptismal candle lit from the flame of the paschal candle and this special prayer was said:
>
> 'Parents, this light is entrusted to you to be kept burning brightly. These children of yours have been enlightened by Christ. They are to walk always as children of the light. Jesus said, "I am the light of the world, whoever follows me will have the light of life and will never walk in darkness."'

If the Presentation of the Gospel takes place during Mass, the Penitential Rite, Gloria (unless in Lent), the opening prayer and the first readings now follow.

Singing of the Alleluia or Gospel acclamation and procession

During the singing of the Gospel acclamation acolytes (carrying lighted candles), followed by the first communion candidates (without candles), and finally the person who is to proclaim the Gospel and is carrying the Lectionary, process to the ambo or lectern. Acolytes stand on either side of the ambo, candidates gather around.

Presider   When we listen to the Gospel stories we ask Our Lord for the light to understand the way he lived his life. Jesus tells us that we must let his light shine through us to others. When we receive him in Holy Communion, Jesus helps us with his strength to become like him, a light for the world.

Gospel reading

This is the Gospel of the Lord…

Homily

During the homily, candidates move to nearby seats or perhaps sit on the floor around the ambo. Adapt according to the size of the group and the local situation.

Presentation of the Scriptures

Presider   *Let us pray for these candidates preparing to receive Our Lord in Holy Communion, that God will fill their hearts with love for the Scriptures they are about to receive.*

> Loving Father, bless these candidates for Eucharist. Through your Holy Spirit enlighten their minds and open their hearts to love and treasure your holy Word. Through the Scriptures they are about to receive may they come to know Jesus and his love for them and the love he wants us to share with each other. We make our prayer through Jesus Christ our Lord. Amen.

Blessing of the books

Presider   We now ask God's blessing on these books of Holy Scripture.

May the blessing of Almighty God, Father, Son and Spirit, come down on these books. May our candidates find in them the living word of God. May these words of Scripture enlighten their minds and fill their hearts with God's love.

(The books are sprinkled with holy water.)

Catechist   In the name of Our Lord and Saviour, Jesus Christ, and in the name of his Church here present, we are happy to invite our candidates to come forward to receive the book which contains the Good News of Jesus Christ.

Invitation to the candidates

Each candidate is invited by name to come forward to receive a copy of the Scriptures.

Catechist   N…*(name of child)*, we invite you to receive the Gospel.

Presider   N…*(name of child)*, receive the Gospel, the Good News of Jesus Christ, the Son of God. Lord, bless this child of light who now receives your Word. May it live always in her/his heart that she/he may bring your light to the world.

Candidate   Thanks be to God.

All   Thanks be to God.

As each child receives a copy of the Scriptures they may be invited to light a candle or night-light in front of the lectern and then remain beside the lectern.

Intercessions

Let us pray for our candidates that the book of God's holy word, which they have received, may enlighten and inspire them to know, love and follow Jesus throughout their lives.

Let us pray that they may learn to listen with their hearts to God speaking to them in the words of Holy Scripture.

Let us pray that God's word may be a living word that speaks to them every day of their lives.

Parents   Lord, bless our children. May the light of Christ always burn brightly in them as they live his word. May they be the light of Christ for others.

(Other intentions may be inserted here.)

Candidates return to their places.

The Mass now continues with the procession of gifts.

Recessional procession

Children may join the recessional procession after the altar servers and in front of the presider. They carry their books held high.

CELEBRATION

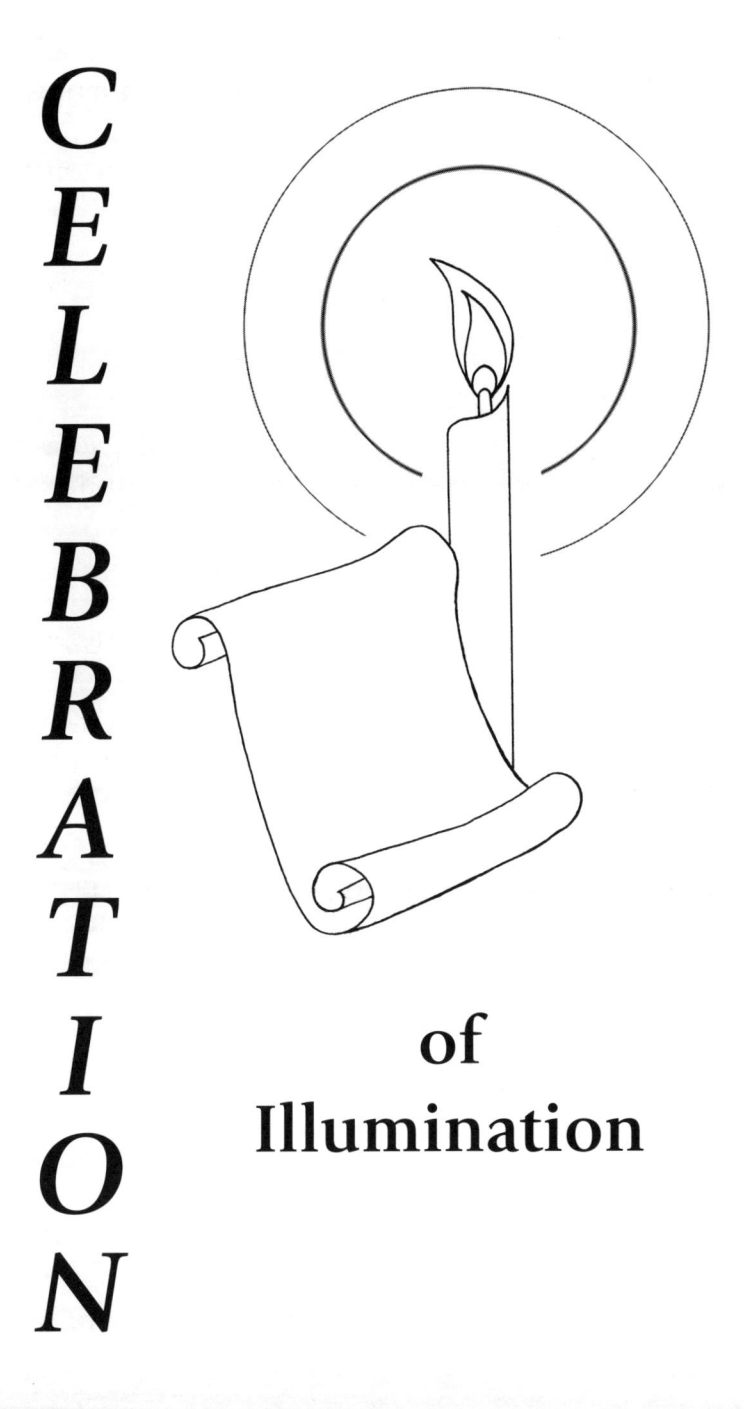

of Illumination

Welcome and introduction

Address to candidates

Gospel acclamation and procession

The candidates will join the Gospel procession after the acolytes. During the proclamation of the Gospel they will stand facing the ambo. During the homily they will move to the nearest seats.

Gospel reading

Presider The Lord be with you.
All And also with you.

Presider A reading from the Holy Gospel…
All Glory to you, Lord.

Homily

Presentation of the Scriptures

Prayer for the candidates

Blessing of the books

Each candidate is invited by name to come forward to receive a book of the Scriptures.

Presider N… *(name of child)*, receive the Gospel, the Good News of Jesus Christ, the Son of God. Lord, bless this child of light who now receives your Word. May it live always in her/his heart, that she/he may bring your light to the world.

Candidate Thanks be to God.

All Thanks be to God.

Intercessions
After the final intercession

Parents Lord, bless our children.
May the light of Christ always burn brightly in them as they live his word.
May they be the light of Christ for others.

Candidates return to their places.

Recessional procession

The Celebration of Tradition

The presentation of the Lord's Prayer

Introduction

As a symbol of the traditions of faith and prayer that parents have handed on to their children since their baptism, they present them with a copy of the Lord's Prayer in this celebration of Tradition.

If celebrated during Mass, the presentation of the Lord's Prayer comes after the homily. It begins with the calling forward of the candidates by name. If it is celebrated outside Mass suitable hymns or music may be included where appropriate.

Preparation

List of names of candidates
Copy of the Lord's Prayer for each candidate
Table on which to place the prayers

For the rite if celebrated outside Mass
Gospel reading
Gathering music or song
Recessional hymn or song

CELEBRATING WITH CHILDREN

The Celebration of Tradition

Introduction

At this celebration the children preparing for their first celebration of Holy Communion will be presented with copies of the Lord's Prayer, the prayer to our Father given to us by Jesus, our Lord. The Lord's Prayer is the most perfect of prayers and is a summary of the whole Gospel. It is at the heart of the Scriptures. It is integral to the sacraments of baptism, confirmation and eucharist. It sums up all we need to pray for in this life and looks eagerly to the coming of God's kingdom and our Lord's return at the end of time.

As Jesus taught his disciples to pray, the parents of these children have taught them to pray. **As a symbol of the traditions of faith and prayer** that these parents have handed on to their children since their baptism, they will today present them with the Lord's Prayer in this celebration of Tradition.

Presider   We welcome to our celebration today our children who are preparing for their first Holy Communion, and their parents. We give thanks for the faith passed on to these children by their parents and which they continue to nourish in them.

If the presentation of the Lord's Prayer takes place during Mass, the Penitential Rite, Gloria (unless in Lent), Opening Prayer, Liturgy of the Word and Homily now follow.

After the homily:

Presider   I now invite our candidates to come forward and to kneel while we pray that they may be filled with a spirit of prayer.

Catechist calls each candidate by name.

Candidates come forward and kneel together in front of the altar.

Presider lays hands on each candidate in turn while the community prays silently.

Presider   Jesus tells us that God is our loving Father and he taught us a beautiful way to pray to God. Jesus said, 'When you pray, call God your Father, say, "Our Father…"' Today we are going to present you with the prayer which Jesus gave us. Parents, I now invite you to come forward to receive the Lord's Prayer which you will present to your children as a symbol of the traditions of faith and prayer which you have handed on to them since their baptism.

Parents come forward to the sanctuary.

Presider   *(To each parent or set of parents.)* I now present you with the Lord's Prayer which you will hand on to your child.

Presider   *(When all the parents have received the Lord's Prayer.)* Candidates, I now invite you to come to your parents to receive the Lord's Prayer.

Children come forward and stand in front of their parents.

Parents   *(Either individually or together.)* N…*(name of child)*, receive the Lord's Prayer. Through it may you always know God as your loving Father.

Presider   Father, we thank you for the way Jesus taught us to pray. We ask that these candidates for Holy Communion, to whom we have presented this prayer, will love and cherish it. Through it may they come to know you as their loving Father and to worship you as the one, true God. May they always turn to you in their needs and seek from you the strength to follow daily Jesus' way of love. We ask this through our Lord Jesus Christ. Amen.

All return to their places.

TRADITION

Intercessions

    Our Father who art in heaven,
        hallowed be thy name.
    May these candidates to whom we
        have presented the Lord's Prayer
    today come to love this prayer and
        to pray it with simple, faithful
        trust.

    Thy kingdom come, thy will be done
        on earth as it is in heaven.
    We pray that God's kingdom may
        grow daily
    in all our lives as we live God's will
        here on earth.

    Give us this day our daily bread.
    We pray that we may always turn
        to God
    in trusting faith and love for all
        our needs
    and that our brothers and sisters
        throughout the world
    may never lack daily bread.

    Forgive us our trespasses
    as we forgive those who trespass
        against us.
    We pray that we may love one
        another as Jesus loves us.
    We pray that we may always have
        hearts ready to forgive.

    And lead us not into temptation.
    We pray that our hearts will always
        be set on God
    like the heart of Mary, Mother of
        God and our Mother.

The Mass now continues with the procession of gifts.

If the presentation takes place outside the Mass:

Presider   Children, you have received the great prayer of God's family. Let us pray this prayer together.

All   Our Father,
    who art in heaven,
    hallowed be thy name;
    thy kingdom come,
    thy will be done
        on earth as it is in heaven.
    Give us this day our daily bread;
    and forgive us our trespasses
    as we forgive those who trespass
        against us;
    and lead us not into temptation
    but deliver us from evil. Amen.

CELEBRATION
of Tradition

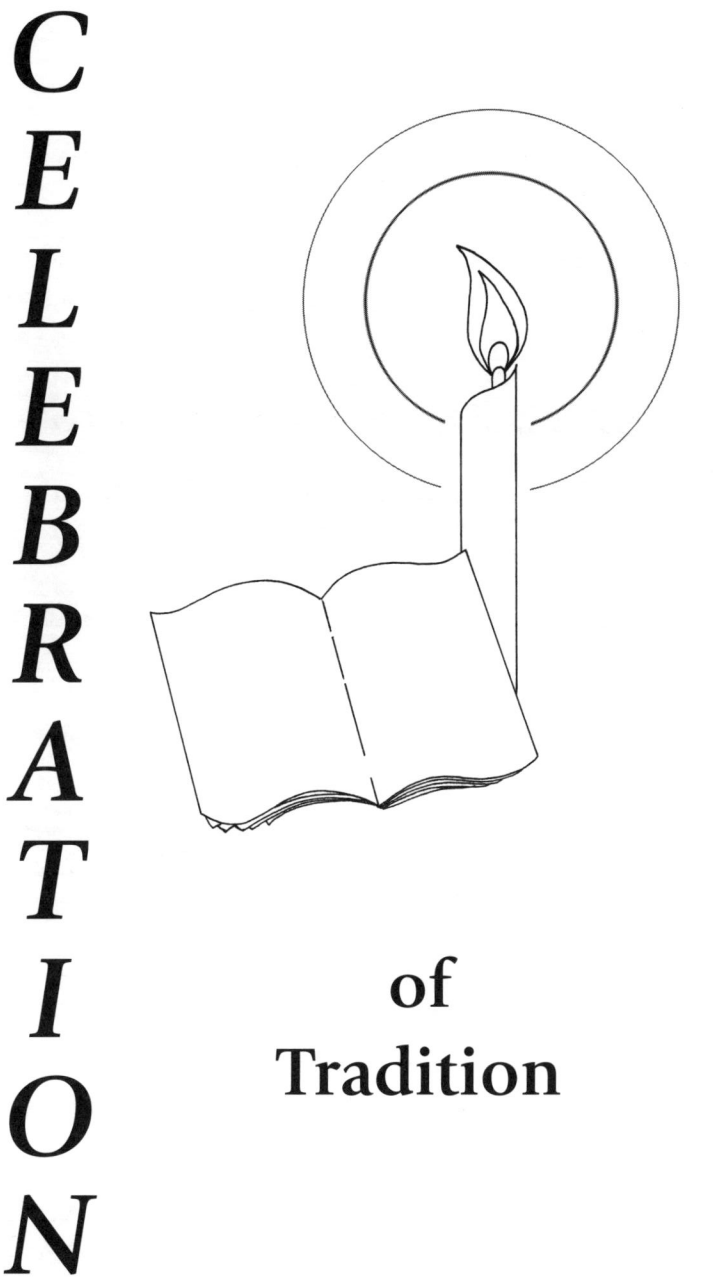

Welcome and introduction

Candidates for first Holy Communion are invited by name to come forward

Candidates come forward and kneel together.

Presider lays hands on each candidate in turn while the community prays silently.

Invitation for the parents of the candidates to come forward

Parents come forward.

Presider   (*to each parent or set of parents*)
I now present you with the Lord's Prayer which you will hand on to your child.

When all the parents have received the Lord's Prayer:

Presider   Candidates, I now invite you to come to your parents to receive the Lord's Prayer.

Parents   (*either individually or together*)
N … (*name of child*), receive the Lord's Prayer. Through it may you always know God as your loving Father.

Presider   Father, we thank you for the way Jesus taught us to pray. We ask that these candidates for Holy Communion, to whom we have presented the prayer which Jesus gave us, will love and cherish it. Through it may they come to know you as their loving Father and to worship you as the one true God. May they always turn to you in their needs and seek from you the strength to follow daily Jesus' way of love. We ask this through Jesus Christ, Our Lord. Amen.

All return to their places.

Intercessions

The Mass continues with the procession of gifts.

If the presentation takes place outside the Mass:

Presider   Children, you have received the great prayer of God's family. Let us pray this prayer together.

All   Our Father, who art in heaven, hallowed be thy name; thy kingdom come, thy will be done on earth as it is in heaven.
Give us this day our daily bread;
and forgive us our trespasses as we forgive those who trespass against us;
and lead us not into temptation but deliver us from evil.
Amen.

CELEBRATION AT THE CRIB

Introduction

Children love the crib. It delights them. They approach it full of awe and wonder, and they never tire of singing the carol, 'Away in a manger'. They know by heart the story of the birth of Jesus in Bethlehem, yet enjoy hearing it over and over again. Children reveal a deep understanding of the nativity in the reverence with which they approach the crib and even illustrations of the nativity on Christmas cards when they point out who is in the scene; 'This is Mary, this is baby Jesus…' The children's own drawings of the nativity are a joy to behold, full of this world and the next. Heaven and earth in one delightful scene. Angels, people, animals, often themselves included, all rejoice together in the children's pictures. Children know that this is not a fairy tale. Children know the Christmas story is true. All of it.

What could be more natural than to gather the children, who are preparing to receive Jesus in sacramental Communion, around the crib to celebrate his birth, together with as many members of their families and the parish community as wish to join them.

Preparation

Choose readers and allocate readings
Invite children to volunteer for the intercessions and let them choose their prayer
Ensure that the words of the carols are available
Choose additional carols as needed

Provide
Night-lights
Containers for night-lights
Tapers and matches
Service leaflets

Celebration at the Crib

Gathering and welcome

Gather the children around the crib. Welcome them to the celebration.

Presider	When God came to earth it was as a helpless little baby. Born, not in a rich, warm and comfortable house, but in a cold, dark stable. Mary wrapped the baby up and laid him in a manger.
Carol	'Come, come, come to the manger.'
Reader	In the fields nearby the shepherds were keeping watch over their sheep. It was very dark. Suddenly the sky was filled with light. The shepherds were afraid. They heard a voice saying, 'Do not be afraid, I bring you good news of great joy. This night a saviour has been born. He is Christ the Lord. You will find the baby wrapped in swaddling clothes and lying in a manger.'
Carol	'While shepherds watched their flocks by night.'
Reader	When the angels left them the shepherds said to each other, 'Let us go to Bethlehem and see for ourselves what has happened'. So they hurried on their way and they found the baby lying in the manger.
Carol	'Away in a manger.'
Reader	With the baby were his mother Mary and Joseph.
Presider	Let us pray the Hail Mary.
Carol	'Silent Night.'

Intercessions

Reader	The ox and the ass kept watch in the stable. Lambs slept in the straw. Chickens pecked around for grain and the cockerel crowed at dawn. Little birds built nests in the roof and spiders spun webs in the corners. Mice peeped out from their holes and Mary and Joseph, filled with wonder, gave glory and thanks to God.
Child	If I were the ox in the crib my prayer would be – Dear God, I am a big, slow animal. Give me time to plod, time to eat, time to sleep, time to think and pray.
Child	If I were the ass in the crib my prayer would be – Dear God, you made me strong to carry heavy loads along rough roads. I am proud to be an ass. One day, when this baby is a man, an ass will carry him.
Child	If I were a lamb at the crib my prayer would be – Dear God, I'm glad I am a lamb because you made me. And when this baby is a man he too will be a lamb: The Lamb of God.
Child	If I were a chicken at the crib my prayer would be – Dear God, it is so snug and warm under my mother hen's wings. One day this baby Jesus will want all his friends to be as close to him, as safe as chickens under mother hen's wings.

Child	If I were a bird at the crib my prayer would be –
	Dear God, tiny as I am you would know and miss me if I fell dead from a tree. You made me and I am precious to you.
Child	If I were a spider at the crib my prayer would be –
	Dear God, high in my corner I spin my web beautiful, lacy and light like a decoration on this first Christmas night.
Child	If I were a mouse at the crib my prayer would be –
	Dear God, I'll be so quiet, just let me stay; I don't mind being poor.
Child	If I were a cockerel at the crib my prayer would be –
	Dear God, let me keep watch all through this night until sunrise, and be first to tell the new dawn that Jesus is born. Cock-a-doodle-doo!
Child	For myself, a child at the crib, my prayer is –

Give each child who wishes, the opportunity to make their own prayer here.

After each prayer light a night-light and place it on a tray or stand, or in a jar.

Carol *(of choice)*

Closing prayer:

Presider	Dear God, Father of our Lord Jesus Christ, with hearts filled with joy and love we thank you for sending Jesus into the world to be our brother. May his birth help us to be loving to one another. May we see him in each others' lives. May we call each one our sister and brother. Amen.

Final carol *(of choice)*

CELEBRATION

at the Crib

Gathering and welcome

The children gather around the crib and are welcomed to the celebration.

Introduction

Carol 'Come, come, come to the manger.'

Reader The shepherds…

Carol 'While shepherds watched their flocks by night.'

Reader The angels…

Carol 'Away in a manger.'

Reader The baby…

Presider Let us pray the Hail Mary.

Carol 'Silent Night.'

Reader The stable…

Intercessions

Child If I were the ox in the crib my prayer would be…

Child If I were the ass in the crib my prayer would be…

Child If I were a lamb at the crib my prayer would be…

Child If I were a chicken at the crib my prayer would be…

Child If I were a bird at the crib my prayer would be…

Child If I were a spider at the crib my prayer would be…

Child If I were a mouse at the crib my prayer would be…

Child If I were a cockerel at the crib my prayer would be…

Child For myself, a child at the crib, my prayer is…

Each child who wishes has the opportunity to make their own prayer here.

After each prayer a night-light is lit and placed on a tray or in a jar.

Carol (of choice)

Closing prayer

Final carol (of choice)

Celebrating a Meal with Friends

Introduction

The Passover or Feast of Unleavened Bread is celebrated by the Jewish people as a memorial of God's intervention on their behalf. It is a week-long celebration of being set free after the long years of slavery in Egypt. The Passover meal cannot be eaten alone, it is shared with family, friends, neighbours, which emphasises that one is saved by belonging to the people of God, as a member of a community.

During his time on earth Jesus celebrated many Passovers with his family and friends.

> Now on the first day of Unleavened Bread the disciples came to Jesus to say, 'Where do you want us to make the preparations for you to eat the Passover?' 'Go to so-and-so in the city', Jesus replied, 'and say to him, "The Master says: My time is near. It is at your house that I am keeping the Passover with my disciples."' The disciples did what Jesus told them and prepared the Passover.
>
> During the meal, as they were eating, Jesus took some bread, and when he had said the blessing he broke it and gave it to the disciples. 'Take it and eat; this is my body.' Then he took a cup, and when he had returned thanks he gave it to them. 'Drink all of you from this, for this is my blood, the blood of the covenant, which is to be poured out for many for the forgiveness of sins.'
>
> Mark 14:12-16, 22-26.

We call the last Passover meal which Jesus shared with the disciples the Last Supper. Every eucharist is a memorial of the supper Jesus shared with his disciples, not however in the sense of an anniversary. Each time the words of Jesus, 'this is my body', 'this is my blood' are pronounced in the Mass, they effect here and now what they express. In this sense there is no difference between one Mass and another.

> On the night he was betrayed, he took bread and gave you thanks and praise. He broke the bread, gave it to his disciples and said: 'Take this, all of you, and eat it: this is my body which will be given up for you.'
>
> Eucharistic prayer 3. Holy Thursday.
> *Roman Missal.*

Jesus is the new Passover Lamb. Jesus is the Lamb of God who takes away the sins of the world.

By celebrating the Last Supper with his apostles in the course of the Passover meal, Jesus gave the Jewish Passover its definitive meaning. Jesus' passing over to his Father by his death and resurrection, the new Passover, is anticipated in the Supper and celebrated in the eucharist, which fulfils the Jewish Passover and anticipates the final Passover of the Church in the glory of the kingdom.
CCC 1340

Preparation

Prepare and send invitations to the families of the candidates for first Communion, their prayer companions or sponsors, catechists, parish clergy, musicians, other helpers.

The Seder Table
On this table arrange:
unleavened bread, boiled egg, bitter herbs (horse radish, watercress), saltwater, lamb bone, chopped apple mixed with cinnamon, honey, nuts and dates, sweet red wine

The Second Table
Communion wine, chalices, ciborium, altar breads

Each family prepares:
name card and place setting for each person they have invited to the meal; a candle for their table; a prayer for their family; a Gospel story for their candidate for Holy Communion

You will also need:
matches, tapers, music and suitable hymns as desired, sweet red wine or grape juice for the four ceremonial cups

The meal can take the form of a shared table or each family can provide their own main course and drinks extra for guests, with a shared desert table, also some sweets for the children.

A Meal with Friends

Welcome

All pause for a moment of quietness to prepare for the meal about be shared.

When Jesus was on earth he shared many meals with his family and friends. Today we are going to remember one very special meal which Jesus shared with his family and friends every year: the feast of Passover. Jewish people still celebrate this feast, remembering how God set the people of Israel free from slavery in Egypt. Moses was the man chosen by God to lead the people into freedom. When the Egyptian Pharaoh refused to free the people of Israel awful things began to happen in Egypt. Plagues of flies and locusts, frogs and darkness and other horrible things descended on the land, but still the Pharaoh refused to set the people of Israel free. Eventually, God said that the eldest son of every family would die on a certain night, unless the family signed their door post with the blood of a sacrificed lamb.

The people of Israel sacrificed a lamb, they signed their door posts with its blood. Dressed ready to set out on a journey, they hurriedly ate their meal. The avenging angel passed over the homes signed with the blood of the lamb. The first-born sons of Israel were saved. At last the Pharaoh set the people of Israel free. They had to leave Egypt very quickly, they did not even have time to wait for their bread to rise, and to this day, in memory of their hasty departure, unleavened bread is still eaten at Passover. A lamb bone is a reminder of the sacrificed lamb whose blood marked the door posts of the people of Israel. Bitter herbs, dipped in salt, are eaten to remind everyone of the bitterness and tears of slavery. Apples mixed with spices, nuts and dates are a symbol of the bricks and mortar the people were forced to make during their time of slavery in Egypt. Eggs are a symbol of new life, and wine of joy and celebration. For the Jewish people the Passover is a great celebration of freedom.

The Last Supper

The last time Jesus shared the Passover meal with his friends we call the 'Last Supper'. At the Last Supper Jesus took the unleavened bread in his hands, gave thanks to God, blessed and broke it and said,

'Take this, all of you, and eat it:
This is my body which will be given up for you.'

When the supper was ended Jesus took the cup of wine, gave God thanks and praise, gave the cup to his disciples and said:

'Take this, all of you, and drink from it:
This is the cup of my blood.
It will be shed for all so that sins may be forgiven.
Do this in memory of me.'

Each time we come together to celebrate Mass we take part in our Lord's own sacrifice of praise and thanksgiving. Jesus is the Lamb of God who takes away the sin of the world.

Lighting the family candles

A parent lights their family candle and either parent or first Communion candidate reads their family prayer.

Blessing the wine

First Communion candidates come forward to receive a glass of wine which they take back to their families.

As a sign of family oneness all hold hands and sing: 'Blest are you, Lord, God of all creation.' (Kevin Mayhew, *Celebration for everyone*)

All   We thank you for your gift of life.

They drink the wine.

The second cup of wine is poured but not drunk.

The question

Parent or
presider   Why do we eat unleavened bread and bitter herbs and salt?

Because at this meal we remember how God set the people of Israel free from the bitterness of slavery.

We remember how they left quickly without waiting for their bread to rise.

Blessing the wine

As a sign of family oneness, all hold hands and sing: 'Blest are you, Lord, God of all creation.'

All   We thank you for the gift of freedom.

They drink the second cup of wine.

Blessing the bread

First Communion candidates come forward to receive some unleavened bread which they take back to their families. One piece of the bread is taken away and hidden.

As a sign of family oneness all hold hands and sing: 'Blest are you, Lord God of all creation.'

All   We thank you for your gift of bread.

The bread is shared and eaten with bitter herbs dipped in the salt water.

The meal is now served.

After the meal

The children find the hidden bread.

Blessing the wine

The third glass of wine is poured.

As a sign of family oneness all hold hands and sing: 'Peace perfect peace, is the gift of Christ our Lord.' (Kevin Mayhew, *Celebration for everyone*)

All   We thank you for your gift of peace.

All share the sign of peace and drink the wine.

The rite of the word

The children share some of their favourite stories about Jesus.

Thanksgiving

All   Lord, we thank you for your wonderful gift of love.
We are happy to be your family, and now, Lord, we thank you for each member of each family.

First Communion candidates name each member of their family.

All   May we always walk together as the family of God.
May we grow in our faith as brothers and sisters and in God's love.
Together may we continue to prepare our children
for their first celebration of Holy Communion.

Communion practice

A parent from each family comes forward to receive an unconsecrated host.

Presider   Parents, you will be the first to show your children how to receive Jesus in Holy Communion, how to hold their hands out reverently in the form of a cross to receive our Lord under the appearance of bread, or how to join their hands and communicate by mouth if that is their choice.
     You will show them how to respond to the invitation 'The Body of Christ,' by saying 'Amen' clearly. Also show your children how to hold and how to drink from the chalice if they wish to receive our Lord under the appearance of wine, and again how to respond 'Amen'.

All pause for a moment in silence to call to mind what we believe in our hearts when we receive our blessed Lord in Holy Communion. Parents might like to share their belief with their children before they practise.

Presider   (*to the children*) At this practice, the bread and wine has not yet been consecrated. The priest has not prayed for the Holy Spirit to come upon it and make it holy so that it may become for us the body and blood of our Lord Jesus Christ, or pronounced the words of consecration: 'This is my body . . . this is my blood'.

CELEBRATING WITH CHILDREN

When the families are ready the parents come forward to receive a host. They then return with it to their child.

Parents and children then come forward to practise with the chalice and wine.

When all are seated…

Blessing the wine
The fourth glass of wine is poured.

As a sign of family oneness all hold hands and sing: 'Praise him, praise him.' (Kevin Mayhew, *Celebration for everyone*)

All   We lift this cup up with love and gratitude to God
for all the blessings given to us as we pray for the future.

They drink the wine.

Final blessing

Presider   Mothers, bow your heads and pray for God's blessing.

May God, the giver of all joy, bless you.
May you always see the light of hope shining in the eyes of your children.
May you always thank God for their presence in your life.

Fathers, bow your heads and pray for God's blessing.

May God, the giver of all life, bless you.
May you always give life and hope to your children by what you say and do.

Children, bow your heads and pray for God's blessing.

May God always bless you with peace and joy.
May you continue to grow in love for God and your families.

Conclude with a hymn or song of choice

CELEBRATING a Meal with Friends

All   May we always walk together as the family of God.
       May we grow in our faith as brothers and sisters and in God's love. Together may we continue to prepare our children for their first celebration of Holy Communion.

Communion practice

Presider explains that this is a practice with unconsecrated elements.

A parent from each family comes forward to receive an unconsecrated host. After practising with the host, parents and children then come forward to practise with the chalice and wine.

When all are seated….

Blessing the wine

The fourth glass of wine is poured.

As a sign of family oneness all hold hands and sing: 'Praise him, praise him.'

All   We lift this cup up with love and gratitude to God for all the blessings given to us as we pray for the future.

They drink the wine.

Final blessing

Presider   Mothers, bow your heads and pray for God's blessing.
            Fathers, bow your heads and pray for God's blessing.
            Children, bow your heads and pray for God's blessing.

Conclude with a hymn or song of choice.

Welcome and introduction

Lighting the family candles
A parent lights their family candle and either parent or first Communion candidate reads their family prayer.

Blessing the wine
First Communion candidates come forward to receive a glass of wine which they take back to their families.

As a sign of family oneness all hold hands and sing: 'Blest are you, Lord, God of all creation.'

All   We thank you for your gift of life.

They drink the wine.

The second cup of wine is poured but not drunk.

The question

Blessing the wine
As a sign of family oneness, all hold hands and sing: 'Blest are you, Lord, God of all creation.'

All   We thank you for the gift of freedom.

They drink the second cup of wine.

Blessing the bread
First Communion candidates come forward to receive some unleavened bread which they take back to their families. One piece of the bread is taken away and hidden.

As a sign of family oneness all hold hands and sing: 'Blest are you, Lord God of all creation.'

All   We thank you for your gift of bread.

The bread is shared and eaten with bitter herbs dipped in the salt water.

The meal is now served.

After the meal

The children find the hidden bread.

Blessing the wine
The third glass of wine is poured.

As a sign of family oneness all hold hands and sing: 'Peace perfect peace, is the gift of Christ our Lord.'

All   We thank you for your gift of peace.

All share the sign of peace and drink the wine.

The Rite of the Word

Candidates share some of their favourite stories about Jesus.

Thanksgiving

All   Lord, we thank you for your wonderful gift of love. We are happy to be your family. Now, Lord, we thank you for each member of each family.

First Communion candidates name each member of their family.

BENEDICTION OF THE BLESSED SACRAMENT

Introduction

'Where two or three are gathered in my name I am with you'.

> While they were at supper Jesus took some bread, and when he had given thanks, broke it and gave it to his disciples, saying, 'This is my body which will be given for you; do this as a memorial of me'. He did the same with the wine after supper, and said, 'This cup is the new covenant in my blood which will be poured out for you'.
>
> Luke 22:19-20.

Taking the bread and wine Jesus gave thanks to the Father. Only through Christ, with him and in him can we offer the sacrifice of praise to God. The bread and wine, the fruits of the earth, all our labour and work, the whole of creation become an offering of praise and thanks to God in the Mass through the power of the Holy Spirit working in the risen Christ.

> Through him, with him, in him,
> in the unity of the Holy Spirit,
> all glory and honour are yours almighty Father,
> forever and ever. Amen.
>
> (Order of Mass)

United in Christ we come together, not passively, but actively, before the blessed sacrament, to give God thanks and praise in Christ for the many gifts of creation. To be people of praise; to become more aware of our responsibility as a community to enter into the redeeming work of Christ; to build a better world. And while we work and while we wait we do so with hope in our hearts, for Christ is risen, he will not leave us orphans, he is with us, in our midst, until the end of time.

Preparation

It is presumed that the sacristan will prepare what is needed for this celebration, for example the altar, monstrance, and thurible; incense, charcoal, matches and candles.

The altar may be decorated with flowers.

An outline service sheet is provided which you can complete by adding your own choice of hymns and a scripture reading.

The congregation will need hymn books.

Suggested readings
Mark 14:12-16, 22:26; John 6:51, 15:9-11.

Suggested hymns

First hymn
'We are gathering together unto him.' Anon

'I am the bread of life.' David Konstant

'Holy, holy, holy, holy.' Jimmy Owens

'Let all that is within me cry holy.' Traditional

Second hymn
'Let there be love shared among us.' Dave Bilbrough

'A new commandment I give unto you.' Anon

'Bind us together, Lord.' Bob Gillman

Third hymn
'Be still for the presence of the Lord.' David J Evans

'Be still and know that I am with you.' Annie Scott

Fourth hymn
'Shine, Jesus, shine.' Graham Kendrick

'Praise him, praise him.' Anon

'Praise the Lord and sing hallelujah.' Gerald O'Mahony

Benediction of the Blessed Sacrament

Exposition
When the people have gathered a song may be sung while the minister comes to the altar and places the blessed sacrament in the monstrance.

Hymn

Adoration

Scripture readings, songs and prayers direct our attention to the worship of Christ the Lord and help to deepen our understanding of the mystery of the eucharist.

Scripture reading

Homily

Hymn

Quiet adoration

Incensing of the blessed sacrament

During the incensing of the sacrament a hymn may be sung.

Presider   Let us pray.

> Lord Jesus Christ,
> May this sacrament of new life fill
>   our hearts with your love, and joy,
> and make us eager for the everlasting
>   joy of your kingdom
> where you live with the Father and
>   the Holy Spirit,
> one God, for ever and ever. Amen.

Blessing

After the prayer the Presider now makes the sign of the cross in silence over the people with the blessed sacrament in the monstrance. The blessed sacrament is then replaced in the tabernacle.

Closing hymn

CELEBRATION

of Benediction
of the Blessed
Sacrament

Exposition

When the people have gathered a song may be sung while the minister comes to the altar and places the blessed sacrament in the monstrance.

Hymn

Adoration

Scripture readings, songs and prayers direct our attention to the worship of Christ the Lord and help to deepen our understanding of the mystery of the eucharist.

Scripture reading

Homily

Hymn

Quiet adoration

Incensing of the sacrament

During the incensing of the sacrament a hymn may be sung.

Presider   Let us pray.

Lord Jesus Christ,
May this sacrament of new life fill our hearts with your love, and joy, and make us eager for the everlasting joy of your kingdom where you live with the Father and the Holy Spirit, one God, for ever and ever. Amen.

Blessing

The presider now makes the sign of the cross in silence over the people with the blessed sacrament in the monstrance. The blessed sacrament is then replaced in the tabernacle.

Closing hymn

Celebration of Praise

Introduction

Having received Christ for the first time in sacramental communion the new communicants are presented with their First Communion certificates at a Mass celebrated at a later date. The certificates are more than a memento of a great day, rather they signify that these children have begun a new stage in the journey of faith with the reception of Holy Communion. It is important to continue to help the children understand the relationship between liturgy and life because, as members of the community, they share in the important ministry of the people of God.

Participation in the eucharistic meal signifies complete integration into the community of believers, full participation in the life, faith and mission of the community, the people of the new covenant; people called to praise God; people entrusted with the mission of raising the whole of creation towards God in praise and thanksgiving; people called to bring about the kingdom proclaimed by Christ and offer it to God through Christ in the eucharist; people who, through lives lived in union with Christ, are signs, even by their smallest efforts, of the new creation.

> Therefore, if anyone is in Christ, there is a new creation, the old one has passed away, behold, the new has come. All this is from God, who through Christ reconciled us to himself and gave us the ministry of reconciliation.
> 2 Corinthians 5:17

When we, the Church, celebrate the eucharist and proclaim the Word of God, we place ourselves at the service of all peoples in order to carry out our Lord's work; he who said,

> 'I came that they may have life and have it to the full.' John 10:10

It is with this life that the new communicants are now in full communion. It is in this mission that they share.

The Mass concludes with the Rite of Dismissal. 'Go in peace to love and serve the Lord', or, at least: 'Go in peace'. We are sent forth to do good works, praising and blessing God, to take Christ's peace to the world.

> Holy Mass (Missa) is one of the names we give to the eucharist, because the liturgy in which the mystery of salvation is accomplished, concludes with the sending forth (mission) of the faithful, so that they may fulfil God's will in their daily lives.
> CCC 1332

Preparation

You will need:
> *A certificate of First Holy Communion for each child with their details filled in.*

The presentation of the Communion certificates takes place during Mass as the children are now fully initiated and can participate fully in the eucharistic meal.

The Mass can be that of the Sunday, or you may want to prepare a Mass with special readings and prayers and a choice of music and hymns.

There is no special service booklet for this celebration as the Mass takes its usual form until after Communion.

CELEBRATING WITH CHILDREN

Celebration of Praise

Greeting

(Theme of the Mass) In the following or similar words:

(Presider) This week we welcome again our new communicants who during this Mass will be presented with their First Communion certificates, signifying that they are now ready to set out on a new stage in their journey of faith, begun with their reception of Holy Communion. With them we celebrate the beginning of the next stage of this journey, the call to live out in full communion with the Church, the following of Christ, according to their ability, and so to share in the mission of the Church.

The Mass continues in its usual form. At the Homily more can be said about the mission of the Church.

The Prayer of the Faithful

Presider   As people called to praise God and entrusted with the mission of raising the whole of creation towards God in praise and thanksgiving, let us now offer our prayers for our own needs and the needs of the world.

Reader   Let us pray for our new communicants and their families, that filled with the love of God they may begin to build a better world through the family love they share with each other.

All   Lord, in your love and kindness hear our prayer.

Reader   Let us pray for our holy Father (N…), and all the members of the Church. May we never cease to remember at every eucharist we celebrate that we are the Body of Christ called to give glory and praise to God.

All   Lord, in your love and kindness hear our prayer.

Reader   Let us pray that as stewards entrusted with the earth, God's gift to us, we will always work towards a just sharing of the world's resources.

All   Lord, in your love and kindness hear our prayer.

Reader   Let us pray for all who are suffering at this time, that God will comfort and strengthen them in their time of need.

All   Lord, in your love and kindness hear our prayer.

Reader   Let us pray for our deceased relatives and friends that they are now the beloved of God in the kingdom prepared for them.

All   Lord, in your love and kindness hear our prayer.

Presider   God, the Father of our Lord Jesus Christ, we bring our prayers before you and ask you to help us to make this world a better place by sharing your love with everyone we meet. We make our prayer in the name of Jesus who together with the Holy Spirit lives with us now and forever. Amen.

Other intercessions may be added if needed.

Concluding rite *(after Communion)*

Distribution of certificates to the new communicants.

Each new communicant is called by name to come forward to the Presider to receive their certificate. The communicants remain either in the sanctuary or nearby until all the certificates have been distributed.

**The Presider prays over
the new communicants:**
> God of all love and goodness, we praise and thank you for the gift of the eucharist given to us by Jesus, your Son, on the night before he died. Thank you for inviting these children to share fully this gift of love, and strengthened by this sacrament may they always faithfully love and serve you, and take the Good News of the kingdom to everyone they meet. We make our prayer through Jesus Christ, our Lord, and the Spirit who lives in our hearts.

The community may now congratulate the new communicants.

Blessing and dismissal